William Henry Harrison Murray

**How John Norton the trapper kept his Christmas**

William Henry Harrison Murray

**How John Norton the trapper kept his Christmas**

ISBN/EAN: 9783742832962

Manufactured in Europe, USA, Canada, Australia, Japa

Cover: Foto ©ninafisch / pixelio.de

Manufactured and distributed by brebook publishing software (www.brebook.com)

William Henry Harrison Murray

## How John Norton the trapper kept his Christmas

*How John Norton the Trapper Kept His Christmas*

William Henry Harrison Murray

# HOW

# JOHN NORTON THE TRAPPER KEPT HIS CHRISTMAS

BY

W. H. H. MURRAY

BOSTON:
DE WOLFE, FISKE & CO.
361 AND 365 Washington Street.

## HOW JOHN NORTON THE TRAPPER KEPT HIS CHRISTMAS.

### I.

A CABIN. A cabin in the woods. In the cabin a great fireplace piled high with logs, fiercely ablaze. On either side of the broad hearth-stone a hound sat on his haunches, looking gravely, as only a hound in a meditative mood can, into the glowing fire. In the centre of the cabin, whose every nook and corner was bright with the ruddy firelight, stood a wooden table, strongly built and solid. At the table sat John Norton, poring over a book, — a book large of size, with wooden covers bound in leather, brown with age, and smooth as with the handling of many generations. The whitened head of the old man was bowed over the broad page, on which one hand rested, with the forefinger marking the sentence. A cabin in the woods filled with firelight, a table, a book, an old man studying the book. This was the scene on Christmas Eve. Outside, the earth was white with snow, and in the blue sky above the snow was the white moon.

" It says here," said the Trapper, speaking to himself, " it says here, ' Give to him that lacketh, and from him that hath not, withhold not thine hand.' It be a good sayin' fur sartin ; and the world would be a good deal better off, as I conceit, ef the folks follered the sayin' a leetle more closely." And here the old man paused a moment, and, with his hand still resting on the page, and his forefinger still pointing at the sentence, seemed pondering what he had been reading. At last he broke the silence again, saying,—

" Yis, the world would be a good deal better off, ef the folks in it follered the sayin' ; " and then he added, " There's another spot in the book I'd orter look at to-night ; it's a good ways furder on, but I guess I can find it. Henry says that the furder on you git in the book, the better it grows, and I conceit the boy may be right; for there be a good deal of murderin' and fightin' in the fore part of the book, that don't make pleasant readin', and what the Lord wanted to put it in fur is a good deal more than a man without book-larnin' can understand. Murderin' be murderin', whether it be in the Bible or out of the Bible; and puttin' it in the Bible, and sayin' it was done by the Lord's commandment, don't make it any better. And a good deal of the fightin' they did in the old time was sartinly without reason and ag'in jedgment, specially where they killed the women-folks and the leetle uns." And while the old man had thus been communicating with himself, touching the character of much of the Old Testament, he had been turning the leaves until he had reached the opening chapters of the New, and had come to the description of the Saviour's birth, and the angelic announcement of it on the earth. Here he paused, and began to read. He read as an old man unaccustomed to letters must read, — slowly and with a show of labor, but with perfect contentment as to his progress, and a brightening face.

"This isn't a trail a man can hurry on onless he spends a good deal of his time on it, or is careless about notin' the signs, fur the words be weighty, and a man must stop at each word, and look around awhile, in order to git all the meanin' out of 'em — yis, a man orter travel this trail a leetle slow, ef he wants to see all there is to see on it."

Then the old man began to read: —

"'Then there was with the angels a multitude of the heavenly host,' — the exact number isn't sot down here," he muttered; "but I conceit there may have been three or four hunderd, — 'praisin' God and singin', Glory to God in the highest, and on 'arth, peace to men of good will.' That's right," said the Trapper. "Yis, peace to men of good will. That be the sort

that desarve peace; the other kind orter stand their chances." And here the old man closed the book, — closed it slowly, and with the care we take of a treasured thing; closed it, fastened the clasps, and carried it to the great chest whence he had taken it, putting it away in its place. Having done this, he returned to his seat, and, moving the chair in front of the fire, he looked first at one hound, and then at the other, and said, "Pups, this be Christmas Eve, and I sartinly trust ye be grateful fur the comforts ye have."

He said this deliberately, as if addressing human companions. The two hounds turned their heads toward their master, looked placidly into his face, and wagged their tails.

"Yis, yis, I understand ye," said the Trapper. "Ye both be comfortable, and, I dare say, that arter yer way ye both be grateful, fur, next to eatin', a dog loves the heat, and ye be nigh enough to the logs to be toastin'. Yis, this be Christmas Eve," continued the old man, " and in the settlements the folks be gittin' ready their gifts. The young people be tyin' up the evergreens, and the leetle uns be onable to sleep because of their dreamin'. It's a pleasant pictur', and I sartinly wish I could see the merrymakin's, as Henry has told me of them, some time, but I trust it may be in his own house, and with his own children." With this pleasant remark, in respect to the one he loved so well, the old man lapsed into silence. But the peaceful contentment of his face, as the firelight revealed it, showed plainly that, though his lips moved not, his mind was still active with pleasant thoughts of the one whose name he had mentioned, and whom he so fondly loved. At last a more sober look came to his countenance, — a look of regret, of self-reproach, the look of a man who remembers something he should not have forgotten, — and he said, —

"I ax the Lord to pardin me, that in the midst of my plenty I have forgot them that may be in want. The shanty sartinly looked

open enough the last time I fetched the trail
past the clearin', and though with the help of
the moss and the clay in the bank she might
make it comfortable, yit, ef the vagabond that
be her husband has forgot his own, and desarted
them, as Wild Bill said he had, I doubt ef there
be vict'als enough in the shanty to keep them
from starvin'. Yis, pups," said the old man,
rising, "it'll be a good tramp through the snow,
but we'll go in the mornin', and see ef the
woman be in want. The boy himself said,
when he stopped at the shanty last summer,
afore he went out, that he didn't see how they
was to git through the winter, and I reckon he
left the woman some money, by the way she
follered him toward the boat; and he told me
to bear them in mind when the snow came, and
see to it they didn't suffer. I might as well
git the pack-basket out, and begin to put the
things in't, fur it be a goodly distance, and an
early start will make the day pleasant to the
woman and the leetle uns, ef vict'als be scant

in the cupboard. Yis, I'll git the pack-basket out, and look round a leetle, and see what I can find to take 'em. I don't conceit' it'll make much of a show, fur what might be good fur a man, won't be of sarvice to a woman; and as fur the leetle uns, I don't know ef I've got a single thing but vict'als that'll fit 'em. Lord! ef I was near the settlements, I might swap a dozen skins fur jest what I wanted to give 'em; but I'll git the basket out, and look round and see what I've got."

In a moment the great pack-basket had been placed in the middle of the floor, and the Trapper was busy overhauling his stores to see what he could find that would make a fitting Christmas gift for those he was to visit on the morrow. A canister of tea was first deposited on the table, and, after he had smelled of it, and placed a few grains of it on his tongue, like a connoisseur, he proceeded to pour more than half of its contents into a little bark box, and, having carefully tied the cover, he placed it in the basket.

"The yarb be of the best," said the old man, putting his nose to the mouth of the canister, and taking a long sniff before he inserted the stopple — "the yarb be of the best, fur the smell of it goes into the nose strong as mustard. That be good fur the woman fur sartin, and will cheer her sperits when she be down-hearted; fur a woman takes as naterally to tea as an otter to his slide, and I warrant it'll be an amazin' comfort to her, arter the day's work be over, more specially ef the work had been heavy, and gone sorter crosswise. Yis, the yarb be good fur a woman when things go crosswise, and the box'll be a great help to her many and many a night beyend doubt. The Lord sartinly had women in mind when he made the yarb, and a kindly feelin' fur their infarmities, and, I dare say, they be grateful accordin' to their knowledge."

A large cake of maple-sugar followed the tea into the basket, and a small chest of honey accompanied it.

"That's honest sweetenin'," remarked the Trapper with decided emphasis; "and that is more'n ye can say of the sugar of the settlements, leastwise ef a man can jedge by the stuff they peddle at the clearin'. The bees be no cheats; and a man who taps his own trees, and biles the runnin' into sugar under his own eye, knows what kind of sweetenin' he's gittin'. The woman won't find any sand in her teeth when she takes a bite from that loaf, or stirs a leetle of the honey in the cup she's steepin'."

Some salt and pepper were next added to the packages already in the basket. A sack of flour and another of Indian-meal followed. A generous round of pork, and a bag of jerked venison, that would balance a twenty-pound weight, at least, went into the pack. On these, several large-sized salmon-trout, that had been smoked by the Trapper's best skill, were laid. These offerings evidently exhausted the old man's resources, for, after looking round a while, and searching the cupboard from bottom to top, he returned to the basket, and contemplated it with satisfaction, indeed, yet with a face slightly shaded with disappointment.

"The vict'als be all right," he said, "fur there be enough to last 'em a month, and they needn't scrimp themselves either. But eatin' isn't all, and the leetle uns was nigh on to naked the last time I seed 'em; and the woman's dress, in spite of the patchin', looked as ef it would desart her, ef she didn't keep a close eye on't. Lord! Lord! what shall I do? fur there's room enough in the basket, and the woman and the leetle uns need garments; that is, it's more'n likely they do, and I haven't a garment in the cabin to take 'em."

"Hillo! Hillo! John Norton! John Norton! Hillo!" The voice came sharp and clear, cutting keenly through the frosty air and the cabin walls. "John Norton!"

"Wild Bill!" exclaimed the Trapper. "I sartinly hope the vagabond hasn't been a-drinkin'. His voice sounds as ef he was sober;

but the chances be ag'in the signs, fur, ef he isn't drunk, the marcy of the Lord or the scarcity of liquor has kept him from it. I'll go to the door, and see what he wants. It's sartinly too cold to let a man stand in the holler long, whether he be sober or drunk;" with which remark the Trapper stepped to the door, and flung it open.

"What is it, Wild Bill? what is it?" he called. "Be ye drunk, or be ye sober, that ye stand there shoutin' in the cold with a log cabin within a dozen rods of ye?"

"Sober, John Norton, sober. Sober as a Moravian preacher at a funeral."

"Yer trappin' must have been mighty poor, then, Wild Bill, for the last month, or the Dutchman at the clearin' has watered his liquor by a wrong measure for once. But ef ye be sober, why do ye stand there whoopin' like an Indian, when the ambushment is on-kivered and the bushes be alive with the knaves? Why don't ye come into the cabin, like a sensible man, ef ye be sober? The signs be ag'in ye, Wild Bill; yis, the signs be ag'in ye."

"Come into the cabin!" retorted Bill. "An' so I would mighty lively, ef I could; but the load is heavy, and your path is as slippery as the plank over the creek at the Dutchman's, when I've two horns aboard."

"Load! What load have ye been draggin' through the woods?" exclaimed the Trapper. "Ye talk as ef my cabin was the Dutchman's, and ye was balancin' on the plank at this minit."

"Come and see for yourself," answered Wild Bill, "and give me a lift. Once in your cabin, and in front of your fire, I'll answer all the questions you may ask. But I'll answer no more until I'm inside the door."

"Ye be sartinly sober to-night," answered the Trapper, laughing, as he started down the hill, "fur ye talk sense, and that's more'n a man can do when he talks through the nozzle of a bottle.

"Lord-a-massy!" exclaimed the old man as he stood over the sled, and saw the huge box that was on it. "Lord-a-massy, Bill! what a tug ye must have had! and how ye come to be sober with sech a load behind ye is beyend the reckinin' of a man who has knowed ye nigh on to twenty year. I never knowed ye disapp'int one arter this fashion afore."

"It is strange, I confess," answered Wild Bill, appreciating the humor that lurked in the honesty of the old man's utterance. "It is strange, that's a fact, for it's Christmas Eve, and I ought to be roaring drunk at the Dutchman's this very minit, according to custom; but I pledged him to get the box through jest as he wanted it done, and that I wouldn't touch a drop of liquor until I had done it. And here it is according to promise, for here I am sober, and here is his box."

"H'ist along, Bill, h'ist along!" exclaimed the Trapper, who suddenly became alive with interest, for he surmised whence the box had come. "H'ist along, Bill, I say, and have done with yer talkin', and let's see what ye have got on yer sled. It's strange that a man of your sense will stand jibberin' here in the snow with a roarin' fire within a dozen rods of ye."

Whatever retort Wild Bill may have contemplated, it was effectually prevented by the energy with which the Trapper pushed the sled after him. Indeed, it was all he could do to keep it off his heels, so earnestly did the old man propel it from behind; and so, with many a slip and scramble on the part of Wild Bill, and a continued muttering on the part of the Trapper about the "nonsense of a man's jibberin' in the snow arter a twenty-mile drag, with a good fire within a dozen rods of him," the sled was shot through the doorway into the cabin, and stood fully revealed in the bright blaze of the firelight.

"Take off yer coat and yer moccasins, Wild Bill," exclaimed the Trapper, as he closed the door, "and git in front of the fire; pull out the coals, and set the tea-pot a-steepin'. The yarb will take the chill out of ye better than the pizen of the Dutchman. Ye'll find a haunch of venison in the cupboard that I roasted to-day, and some johnny-cake; I doubt ef either be cold. Help yerself, help yerself, Bill, while I take a peep at the box."

No one can appreciate the intensity of the old man's feelings in reference to the mysterious box, unless he calls to mind the strictness with which he was wont to interpret and fulfil the duties of hospitality. To him the coming of a guest was a welcome event, and the service which the latter might require of the host both a sacred and pleasant obligation. To serve a guest with his own hand, which he did with a natural courtesy peculiar to himself, was his delight. Nor did it matter with him what the quality of the guest might be. The wandering trapper or the vagabond Indian was served with as sincere attention as the richest

visitor from the city. But now his feelings were
so stirred by the sight of the box thus strangely
brought to him, and by his surmise touching who
the sender might be, that Wild Bill was left to
help himself without the old man's attendance.

It was evident that Bill was equal to the
occasion, and was not aware of the slightest
neglect. At least, his actions were not, by the
neglect of the Trapper, rendered less decided, or
the quality of his appetite affected, for the examination he made of the old man's cupboard,
and the familiarity with which he handled the
contents, made it evident that he was not in
the least abashed, or uncertain how to proceed;
for he attacked the provisions with the energy
of a man who had fasted long, and who has at
last not only come suddenly to an ample supply
of food, but also feels that for a few moments,
at least, he will be unobserved. The Trapper
turned toward the box, and approached it for
a deliberate examination.

"The boards be sawed," he said, "and they

come from the mills of the settlement, for the smoothin'-plane has been over 'em." Then he inspected the jointing, and noted how truly the edges were drawn.

"The box has come a goodly distance," he said to himself, "fur there isn't a workman this side of the Horicon that could j'int it in that fashion. There sartinly orter be some letterin', or a leetle bit of writin', somewhere about the chest, tellin' who the box belonged to, and to whom it was sent." Saying this, the old man unlashed the box from the sled, and rolled it over, so that the side might come uppermost. As no direction appeared on the smoothly planed surface, he rolled it half over again. A little white card neatly tacked to the board was now revealed. The Trapper stooped, and on the card read, —

JOHN NORTON,

TO THE CARE OF WILD BILL.

"Yis, the 'J' be his'n," muttered the old man, as he spelled out the word J-o-h-n, "and the big 'N' be as plain as an otter-trail in the snow. The boy don't make his letters over-plain, as I conceit, but the 'J' and the 'N' be his'n." And then he paused for a full minute, his head bowed over the box. "The boy don't forgit," he murmured, and he wiped his eyes with the back of his hand. "The boy don't forgit." And then he added, "No, he isn't one of the forgittin' kind. Wild Bill," said the Trapper, as he turned toward that personage, whose attack on the venison haunch was as determined as ever, "Wild Bill, this box be from Henry!"

"I shouldn't wonder," answered that individual, speaking from a mass of edibles that filled his mouth.

"And it be a Christmas gift!" continued the old man.

"It looks so," returned Bill, as laconically as before.

"And it be a mighty heavy box!" said the Trapper.

"You'd 'a' thought so, if you had dragged it over the mile-and-a-half carry. It was good sleddin' on the river, but the carry took the stuff out of me."

"Very like, very like," responded the Trapper; "fur the gullies be deep on the carry, and it must have been slippery haulin'. Didn't ye git a leetle 'arnest in yer feelin's, Bill, afore ye got to the top of the last ridge?"

"Old man," answered Bill as he wheeled his chair toward the Trapper, with a pint cup of tea in the one hand, and wiping his mustache with the coat-sleeve of the other, "I got it to the top three times, or within a dozen feet from the top, and each time it got away from me and went to the bottom agin; for the roots was slippery, and I couldn't git a grip on the toe of my moccasins; but I held on the rope, and I got to the bottom neck and neck with the sled every time."

"Ye did well, ye did well," responded the Trapper, laughing; "fur a loaded sled goes down-hill mighty fast when the slide is a steep un, and a man who gits to the bottom as quick as the sled must have a good grip, and be considerably in 'arnest. But ye got her up finally by the same path, didn't ye?"

"Yes, I got her up," returned Bill. "The fourth time I went for that ridge, I fetched her to the top, for I was madder than a hornet."

"And what did ye do, Bill?" continued the Trapper. "What did ye do when ye got to the top?"

"I jest tied that sled to a sapling so it wouldn't git away agin, and I got on to the top of that box, and I talked to that gulch a minit or two in a way that satisfied my feelings."

"I shouldn't wonder," answered the Trapper, laughing, "fur ye must have been a good deal riled. But ye did well to git the box through, and ye got here in time, and ye've 'arnt yer wages; and now, ef ye'll tell me how much I am to pay ye, ye shall have yer money, and ye needn't scrimp yourself on the price, Wild Bill, for the drag has been a hard un; so tell me yer price, and I'll count ye out the money."

"Old man," answered Bill, "I didn't bring that box through for money, and I won't take a"—

Perhaps Wild Bill was about to emphasize his refusal by some verbal addition to the simple statement, but, if it was his intention, he checked himself, and said, "a cent."

"It's well said," answered the Trapper; "yis, it's well said, and does jestice to yer feelin's, I don't doubt; but an extra pair of breeches one of these days wouldn't hurt ye, and the money won't come amiss."

"I tell ye, old man," returned Wild Bill earnestly, "I won't take a cent. I'll allow there's several colors in my trousers, for I've patched in a dozen different pieces off and on, and I doubt, as ye hint, if the patching holds together much longer; but I've eaten at your table and slept in your cabin more than once, John Norton, and whether I've come to it sober or drunk, your door was never shut in my face, and I don't forget either that the man who sent you that box fished me from the creek one day, when I had walked into it with two bottles of the Dutchman's whiskey in my pocket, and not one cent of your money or his will I take for bringing the box in to you."

"Have it yer own way, ef ye will," said the Trapper; "but I won't forgit the deed ye have did, and the boy won't forgit it neither. Come, let's clear away the vict'als, and we'll open the box. It's sartinly a big un, and I would like to see what he has put inside of it."

The opening of the box was a spectacle such as gladdens the heart to see. At such moments the countenance of the Trapper was as facile in the changefulness of its expression as that of a child. The passing feelings of his soul found an adequate mirror in his face, as the white

clouds of a summer day find full reflection in
the depth of a tranquil lake. He was not
too old or too learned to be wise, for the wisdom of hearty happiness was his, — the wisdom
of being glad, and gladly showing it.

As for Wild Bill, the best of his nature was
in the ascendant, and with the curiosity and
pleasure of a child, and a happiness as sincere
as if the box was his own, he assisted at the
opening.

"The man who made this box did the work
in a workmanlike fashion," said the Trapper, as
he strove to insert the edge of his hatchet into
the jointing of the cover, "fur he shet these
boards together like the teeth of a bear-trap
when the bars be well 'iled. It's a pity the boy
didn't send him along with the box, Wild Bill,
fur it sartinly looks as ef we should have to
kindle a fire on it, and burn a hole in through
the cover."

At last, by dint of great exertion, and with
the assistance of Wild Bill and the poker, the

cover of the box was wrenched off, and the contents were partially revealed.

"Glory to God, Wild Bill!" exclaimed the Trapper. "Here be yer breeches!" and he held up a pair of pantaloons made of the stoutest Scotch stuff. "Yis, here be yer breeches, fur here on the waistband be pinned a bit of paper, and on it be written, 'Fur Wild Bill.' And here be a vest to match; and here be a jacket; and here be two pairs of socks in the pockets of the jacket; and here be two woollen shirts, one packed away in each sleeve. And here!" shouted the old man, as he turned up the lapel of the coat, "Wild Bill, look here! Here be a five-dollar note!" and the old man swung one of the socks over his head, and shouted, "Hurrah for Wild Bill!" And the two hounds, catching the enthusiasm of their master, lifted their muzzles into the air, and bayed deep and long, till the cabin fairly shook with the joyful uproar of man and dogs.

It is doubtful if any gift ever took the recipient more by surprise than this bestowed upon Wild Bill. It is true that, judged by the law of strict deserts, the poor fellow had not deserved much of the world, and certainly the world had not forgotten to be strictly just in his case, for it had not given him much. It is a question if he had ever received a gift before in all his life, certainly not one of any considerable value. His reception of this generous and thoughtful provision for his wants was characteristic both of his training and his nature.

The old Trapper, as he had ended his cheering, flung the pantaloons, the vest, the jacket, the socks, the shirts, and the money into his lap.

For a moment the poor fellow sat looking at the warm and costly garments that he held in his hands, silent in an astonishment too profound for speech, and then, recovering the use of his organs, he gasped forth, —

"I swear!" and then broke down, and sobbed like a child.

The Trapper, kneeling beside the box, looked at the poor fellow with a face radiant with happiness, while his mouth was stretched with laughter, utterly unconsious that tears were brimming his own eyes.

"Old Trapper," said Wild Bill, rising to his feet, and holding the garments forth in his hands, "this is the first present I ever received in my life. I have been kicked and cussed, sneered at and taunted, and I deserved it all. But no man ever gave me a lift, or showed he cared a cent whether I starved or froze, lived or died. You know, John Norton, what a fool I've been, and what has ruined me, and that when sober I'm more of a man than many who hoot me. And here I swear, old man, that while a button is on this jacket, or two threads of these breeches hold together, I'll never touch a drop of liquor, sick or well, living or dying, so help me God! and there's my hand on it."

"Amen!" exclaimed the Trapper, as he sprang to his feet, and clasped in his own strong palm the hand that the other had stretched out to him. "The Lord in his marcy be nigh ye when tempted, Bill, and keep ye true to yer pledge!"

Of all 'the pleasant sights that the angels of God, looking from their high homes, saw on earth that Christmas Eve, perhaps not one was dearer in their eyes than the spectacle here described, — the two sturdy men standing with their hands clasped in solemn pledge of the reformation of the one, and the helping sympathy of the other, above that Christmas-box in the cabin in the woods.

It is not necessary to follow in detail the Trapper's further examination of the box. The reader's imagination, assisted by many a happy reminiscence, will enable him to realize the scene. There was a small keg of powder, a large plug of lead, a little chest of tea, a bag of sugar, and also one of coffee. There were nails, matches, thread, buttons, a woollen under-jacket, a pair of mittens, and a cap of choicest fur, made of an otter's skin that Henry himself had trapped a year before. All these and other packages were taken out one by one, carefully examined, and characteristically commented on by the Trapper, and passed to Wild Bill, who in turn inspected and commented on them, and then laid them carefully on the table. Beneath these packages was a thin board, constituting a sort of division between its upper and lower half.

"There seems to be a sort of cellar to this box," said the Trapper, as he sat looking at the division. "I shouldn't be surprised ef the boy himself was in here somewhere, so be ready, Bill, fur anything, fur the Lord only knows what's underneath this board." Saying which, the old man thrust his hand under one end of the division, and pulled out a bundle loosely tied with a string, which became unfastened as the Trapper lifted the roll from its place in the box, and, as he shook it open, and held its contents at arm's length up to the light, the startled eyes of Wild Bill, and the earnest gaze of the Trapper, beheld a woman's dress!

"Heavens and 'arth, Bill!" exclaimed the Trapper, "what's this?" And then a flash of light crossed his face, in the illumination of which the look of wonder vanished, and, dropping upon his knees, he flung the dividing board out of the box, and his companion and himself saw at a glance what was underneath.

Children's shoes, and dresses of warmest stuffs; tippets and mittens; a full suit for a little boy, boots and all; a jack-knife and whistle; two dolls dressed in brave finery, with flaxen hair and blue eyes; a little hatchet; a huge ball of yarn, and a hundred and one things needed in the household; and underneath all a Bible; and under that a silver star on a blue field, and pinned to the silk a scrap of paper, on which was written, —

"Hang this over the picture of the lad."

"Ay, ay," said the Trapper in a tremulous

voice, as he looked at the silver star, "it shall be done as ye say, boy; but the lad has got beyend the clouds, and is walkin' a trail that is lighted from eend to eend by a light clearer and brighter than ever come from the shinin' of any star. I hope we may be found worthy to walk it with him, boy, when we, too, have come to the edge of the Great Clearin'."

To the Trapper it was perfectly evident for whom the contents of the box were intended; but the sender had left nothing in doubt, for, when the old man had lifted from the floor the board that he had flung out, he discovered some writing traced with heavy pencilling on the wood, and which without much effort he spelled out to Wild Bill, —

"Give these on Christmas Day to the woman at the dismal hut, and a merry Christmas to you all."

"Ay, ay," said the Trapper, "it shall be did, barrin' accident, as ye say; and a merry Christmas it'll make fur us all. Lord-a-massy! what *will* the poor woman say when she and her leetle uns git these warm garments on? There be no trouble about fillin' the basket now; no, I sartinly can't git half of the stuff in. Wild Bill, I guess ye'll have to do some more sleddin' to-morrow, fur these presents must go over the mountain in the mornin', ef we have to harness up the pups." And then he told his companion of the poor woman and the children, and his intended visit to them on the morrow.

"I fear," he said, "that they be havin' a hard time of it, 'specially ef her husband has deserted her."

"Little good would he do her, if he was with her," answered Wild Bill, "for he's a lazy knave when he's sober, and a thief as well, as you and I know, John Norton; for he's fingered our traps more than once, and swapped the skins for liquor at the Dutchman's; but he's thieved once too many times, for the folks in the settlement has ketched him in the act, and they put him in the jail for six months, as I heard day before yesterday."

"I'm glad on't; yis, I'm glad on't," answered the Trapper; "and I hope they'll keep him there till they've larnt him how to work. I've had my eye on the knave fur a good while, and the last time I seed him I told him ef he fingered any more of my traps, I'd larn him the commandments in a way he wouldn't forgit; and, as I had him in hand, and felt a leetle like talkin' that mornin', I gin him a piece of my mind, techin' his treatment of his wife and leetle uns, that he didn't relish, I fancy, fur he winced and squirmed like a fox in a trap. Yis, I'm glad they've got the knave, and I hope they'll keep him till he's answered fur his misdoin'; but I'm sartinly afeered the poor woman be havin' a hard time of it."

"I fear so, too," answered Wild Bill; "and if I can do anything to help you in your plans, jest say the word, and I'm your man to back or haul, jest as you want me."

And so it was arranged that they should go over the mountain together on the morrow, and take the provisions and the gifts that were in the box to the poor woman; and, after talking awhile of the happiness their visit would give, the two men, happy in their thoughts, and with their hearts full of that peace which passeth the understanding of the selfish, laid themselves down to sleep; and over the two, — the one drawing to the close of an honorable and well-spent life, the other standing at the middle of a hitherto useless existence, but facing the future with a noble resolution, — over the two, as they slept, the angels of Christmas kept their watch.

## II.

On the other side of the mountain stood the dismal hut; and the stars of that blessed eve had shone down upon the lonely clearing in which it stood, and the smooth white surface of the frozen and snow-covered lake which lay in front of it, as brightly as they had shone on the cabin of the Trapper; but no friendly step had made its trail in the surrounding snow, and no blessed gift had been brought to its solitary door.

As the evening wore on, the great clearing round about it remained drearily void of sound or motion, and filled only with the white stillness of the frosty, snow-lighted night. Once, indeed, a wolf stole from underneath the dark balsams into the white silence, and, running up a huge log that lay aslant a ledge of rocks, looked across and round the great opening in the woods, stood a moment, then gave a shivering sort of a yelp, and scuttled back under the shadows of the forest, as if its darkness was warmer than the frozen stillness of the open space. An owl, perched somewhere amid the pine-tops, snug and warm within the cover of its arctic plumage, engaged from time to time in solemn gossip with some neighbor that lived on the opposite shore of the lake. And once a raven, roosting on the dry bough of a lightning-blasted pine, dreamed that the white moonlight was the light of dawn, and began to stir his sable wings, and croak a harsh welcome; but awakened by his blunder, and ashamed of his mistake, he broke off in the very midst of his discordant call, and again settled gloomily down amid his black plumes to his interrupted repose, making by his sudden silence the surrounding silence more silent than before. It seemed as if the very angels, who, we are taught, fly abroad over all the earth that blessed

night, carrying gifts to every household, had forgotten the cabin in the woods, and had left it to the cold hospitality of unsympathetic nature.

Within the lonely hut, which thus seemed forgotten of Heaven itself, sat a woman huddling her young — two girls and a boy. The fireplace was of monstrous proportions, and the chimney yawned upward so widely that one looking up the sooty passage might see the stars shining overhead. A little fire burned feebly in the huge stone recess: scant warmth might such a fire yield, kindled in such a fireplace, to those around it. Indeed, the little flame seemed conscious of its own inability, and burned with a wavering and mistrustful flicker, as if it was discouraged in view of the task set before it, and had more than half concluded to go out altogether.

The cabin was of large size, and undivided into apartments. The little fire was only able to illuminate the central section, and more than half of the room was hidden in utter darkness. The woman's face, which the faint flame over which she was crouched revealed with painful clearness, showed pale and haggard. The induration of exposure and the tightening lines of hunger sharpened and marred a countenance which a happier fortune would have kept even comely. It had that old look about it which comes from wretchedness rather than age, and the weariness of its expression was pitiful to see. Was it work or vain waiting for happier fortunes that made her look so tired? Alas! the weariness of waiting for what we long for, and long for purely, but which never comes! Is it the work or the longing — the long longing — that has put the silver in your head, friend, and scarred the smooth bloom of your cheeks, my lady, with those ugly lines?

"Mother, I'm hungry," said the little boy, looking up into the woman's face. "Can't I have just a little more to eat?"

"Be still," answered the woman sharply,

speaking in the tones of vexed inability. "I've given you almost the last morsel in the house."

The boy said nothing more, but nestled up more closely to his mother's knee, and stuck one little stockingless foot out until the cold toes were half hidden in the ashes. O warmth! blessed warmth! how pleasant art thou to old and young alike! Thou art the emblem of life, as thy absence is the evidence and sign of life's cold opposite. Would that all the cold toes in the world could get to my grate to-night, and all the shivering ones be gathered to this fireside! Ay, and that the children of poverty, that lack for bread, might get their hungry hands into that well-filled cupboard there, too!

In a moment the woman said, "You children had better go to bed. You'll be warmer in the rags than in this miserable fireplace."

The words were harshly spoken, as if the very presence of the children, cold and hungry as they were, was a vexation to her; and they moved off in obedience to her command.

O cursed poverty! I know thee to be of Satan, for I myself have eaten at thy scant table, and slept in thy cold bed. And never yet have I seen thee bring one smile to human lips, or dry one tear as it fell from a human eye. But I have seen thee sharpen the tongue for biting speech, and harden the tender heart. Ay, I've seen thee make even the presence of love a burden, and cause the mother to wish that the puny babe nursing her scant breast had never been born. And so the children went to their unsightly bed, and silence reigned in the hut.

"Mother," said one of the girls, speaking out of the darkness, — "mother, isn't this Christmas Eve?"

"Yes," answered the woman sharply. "Go to sleep." And again there was silence.

Happy is childhood, that amid whatever deprivation and misery it can so weary itself in the day that when night comes on it can lose in the forgetfulness of slumber its sorrows and wants!

Thus, while the children lost the sense of their unhappy surroundings, including the keen pangs of hunger, for a time, and under the tattered blankets that covered them saw, perhaps, visions of enchanting lands, and in their dreams feasted at those wonderful tables which hungry children see only in sleep, to the poor woman sitting at the failing fire there came no surcease of sorrow, and no vision threw even an evanescent brightness over the hard, cold facts of her surroundings. And the reality of her condition was dire enough, God knows. Alone in the wilderness, miles from any human habitation, the trails covered deep with snow, her provisions exhausted, actual suffering already upon them, and starvation staring them squarely in the face. No wonder that her soul sank within her ; no wonder that her thoughts turned toward bitterness.

"Yes, it's Christmas Eve," she muttered, "and the rich will keep it gayly. God sends them presents enough ; but you see if he remembers me! Oh, they may talk about the angels of Christmas Eve flying abroad to-night, loaded with gifts, but they'll fly mighty high above this shanty, I reckon; no, they won't even drop a piece of meat as they soar past." And so she sat muttering and moaning over her woes, and they were heavy enough, — too heavy for her poor soul, unassisted, to lift, — while the flame on the hearth grew thinner and thinner, until it had no more warmth in it than the shadow of a ghost, and, like its resemblance, was about to flit and fade away. At last she said, in a softened tone, as if the remembrance of the Christmas legend had softened her surly thoughts and sweetened the bitter mood, —

"Perhaps I'm wrong to take on so. Perhaps it isn't God's fault that I and my children are deserted and starving. But why should the innocent be punished for the guilty, and why should the wicked have enough and to spare, while those who do no evil go half naked and starved?"

Alas, poor woman! that puzzle has puzzled many besides thee, and many lips besides thine have asked that question, querulously or entreatingly, many a time; but whether they asked it in vexation and rebellion of spirit, or humbly besought Heaven to answer, to neither murmur nor prayer did Heaven vouchsafe a response. Is it because we are so small, or, being small, are so inquisitive, that the Great Oracle of the blue remains so dumb when we cry?

At this point the poor little flame, as if unable to abide the cold much longer, flared fitfully, and uneasily shifted itself from brand to brand, threatening with many a flicker to go out; but the woman, with her elbows on her knees, and her face settled firmly between her hands, still sat with eyes that saw not the feeble flame at which they so steadily gazed.

"I will do it, *I will do it!*" she suddenly exclaimed. "I will make one more effort. They shall not starve while I have strength to try. Perhaps God will aid me. They say he always does at the last pinch, and he certainly sees that I am there now. I wonder if he's been waiting for me to get just where I am before he helped me? There is one more chance left, and I'll make the trial. I'll go down to the shore where I saw the big tracks in the snow. It's a long way, but I shall get there somehow. If God is going to be good to me, he won't let me freeze or faint on the way. Yes, I'll creep into bed now, and try and get a little sleep, for I must be strong in the morning." And with these words the poor woman crept off to her bed, and burrowed down, more like an animal than a human being, beside her little ones, as they lay huddled close together and asleep, down in the rags.

What angel was it that followed her to her miserable couch, and stirred kindly feelings in her bosom? Some sweet one, surely; for she shortly lifted herself to a sitting posture, and, gently drawing down the old blanket with

which the children, for warmth's sake, had
wrapped their heads, looked as only a mother
might at the three little faces lying side by
side, and, bending tenderly over them, she
placed a gentle kiss upon the forehead of each;
then she nestled down again in her own place,
and said, "Perhaps God will help me." And
with this sentence, half a prayer and half a
doubt, born on the one hand from that sweet
faith which never quite deserts a woman's
bosom, and on the other from that bitter experience which had made her seem in her own
eyes deserted of God, she fell asleep.

She, too, dreamed; but her dreaming was
only the prolongation of her waking thoughts;
for long after her eyes closed she moved uneasily
on her hard couch, and muttered, " Perhaps God
will. Perhaps " —

Sad is it for us who are old enough to have
tasted the bitterness of that cup which life
sooner or later presents to all lips, and have
borne the burden of its toil and fretting, that

our vexations and disappointments pursue us even in our slumber, disturbing our sleep with reproachful visions and the sound of voices whose upbraiding robs us of our otherwise peaceful repose. Perhaps somewhere in the years to come, after much wandering and weariness, guided of God, we may come to that fountain of which the ancients dreamed, and for which the noblest among them sought so long, and died seeking; plunging into which, we shall find our lost youth in its cool depths, and, rising refreshed and strengthened, shall go on our eternal journey re-clothed with the beauty, the innocence, and the happiness of our youth.

The poor woman slept uneasily, and with much muttering to herself; but the rapid hours slid noiselessly down the icy grooves of night, and soon the cold morning put its white face against the frozen windows of the east, and peered shiveringly forth. Who says the earth cannot look as cold and forbidding as the human countenance? The sky hung over the frozen world like a dome of gray steel, whose invisibly matched plates were riveted here and there by a few white, gleaming stars. The surface of the snow sparkled with crystals that flashed colorlessly cold. The air seemed armed, and full of sharp, eager points that pricked the skin painfully. The great tree-trunks cracked their sharp protests against the frosty entrances being made beneath their bark. The lake, from under the smothering ice, roared in dismay and pain, and sent the thunders of its wrath at its imprisonment around the resounding shores. A bitter morn, a bitter morn, — ah me! a bitter morn for the poor!

The woman, wakened by the gray light, moved in the depths of the tattered blankets, sat upright, rubbed her eyes with her hands, looked about her as if to recall her scattered senses, and then, as thought returned, crept stealthily out of the hole in which she had lain, that she might not wake the children, who, coiled together, slumbered on, still closely clasped in the arms of blessed unconsciousness.

"They had better sleep," she said to herself. "If I fail to bring them meat, I hope they will never wake!"

Ah! if the poor woman could only have foreseen the bitter disappointment, or that other something which the future was to bring her, would she have made that prayer? Is it best for us, as some say, that we cannot see what is coming, but must weep on till the last tear is shed, uncheered by the sweet fortune so nigh, or laugh unchecked until the happy tones are mingled with, and smothered by, the rising moan? Is it best, I wonder?

She noiselessly gathered together what additions she could make to her garments, and then, taking down the rifle from its hangings, opened the door, and stepped forth into the outer cold. There was a look of brave determination in her eyes as she faced the chilly greeting the world gave her, and with more

## JOHN NORTON'S CHRISTMAS.

of hopefulness than had before appeared upon her countenance, she struck bravely off along the lake shore, which at this point receded toward the mountain.

For an hour she kept steadily on, with her eyes constantly on the alert for the least sign of the wished and prayed-for game. Suddenly she stopped, and crouched down in the snow, peering straight ahead. Well might she seek concealment, for there, standing on a point of land that jutted sharply out into the lake, not forty rods away, unscreened and plain to view, stood a buck of such goodly proportions as one even in years of hunting might not see.

The woman's eyes fairly gleamed as she saw the noble animal standing thus in full sight; but who may tell the agony of fear and hope that filled her bosom! The buck stood lordly erect, facing the east, as if he would do homage to, or receive homage from, the rising sun, whose yellow beams fell full upon his uplifted front. The thought of her mind, the fear of her heart, were plain. The buck would soon move; when he moved, which way would he move? Would he go from or come toward her? Would she get him, or would she lose him? Oh, the agony of that thought!

"God of the starving," burst from her quivering lips, "let not my children die!"

Many prayers more ornate rose that day to Him whose ears are open to all cries. But of all that prayed on that Christmas morn, whether with few words or many, surely, no heart rose with the seeking words more earnestly than the poor woman kneeling as she prayed, rifle in hand, amid the snow.

"God of the starving, let not my children die!"

That was her prayer; and, as if in answer to her agonizing petition, the buck turned and began to advance directly toward her, browsing as he came. Once he stopped, looked around, and snuffed the air suspiciously. Had he scented her presence, and would he bound away? Should she fire now? No; her judgment told her she could not trust the gun or her aim at such a range. He must come nigher, — come even to the big maple, and stand there, not ten rods away; then she felt sure she should get him. So she waited. Oh, how the cold ate into her! How her teeth chattered as the chills ran their torturing courses through her thin, shivering frame! But still she clutched the cold barrel, and still she watched and waited, and still she prayed, —

"God of the starving, let not my children die!"

Alas, poor woman! My own body shivers as I think of thine, and my pen falters to write what misery befell thee on that wretched morn.

Did the buck turn? Did he, having come so tantalizingly near, retrace his steps? No. He continued to advance. Had Heaven heard her prayer? Her soul answered it had; and with such feelings in it toward Him to whom she had appealed as she had not felt in all her life before, she steadied herself for the shot. For even as she prayed, the deer came on, — came to the big maple, and lifted his muzzle to its highest reach to seize with his tongue a thin streamer of moss that lay against the smooth bark. There he stood, his blue-brown side full toward her, unconscious of her presence. Noiselessly she cocked the piece. Noiselessly she raised it to her face, and with every nerve drawn to its tightest tension, sighted the noble game, and — *fired.*

Had the frosty air watered her eye? was it a tear of joy and gratitude that dimmed the clearness of its sight? or were the half-frozen fingers unable to steady the cold barrel at the instant of its explosion? We know not. We only know that in spite of prayer, in spite of noblest effort, she missed the game. For,

as the rifle cracked, the buck gave a snort of fear, and with swift bounds flew up the mountain; while the poor woman, dropping the gun with a groan, fell fainting on the snow.

## III.

At the same moment the rifle sounded, two men, the Trapper with his pack, and Wild Bill with his sled heavily loaded, were descending the western slope of the mountain, not a mile from the clearing in which stood the lonely cabin. The sound of the piece brought them to a halt as quickly as if the bullet had cut through the air in front of their faces. For several minutes both stood in the attitude of listening.

"Down into the snow with ye, pups!" exclaimed the Trapper, in a hoarse whisper. "Down into the snow with ye, I say! Rover, ef ye lift yer muzzle agin, I'll warm yer back with the ramrod. By the Lord, Bill, the buck is comin' this way; ye can see his horns lift above the leetle balsams as he breaks through

the thicket yender. Ef he strikes the runway, he'll sartinly come within range;" and the old Trapper slipped his arms from the pack, and, lowering it to the earth, sank on his knees beside it, where he waited as motionless as if the breath had departed his body.

Onward came the game. As the Trapper had suggested, the buck, with mighty and far-reaching bounds, cleared the shrubby obstructions, and, entering the runway, tore up the familiar path with the violence of a tornado. Onward he came, his head flung upward, his antlers laid well back, tongue lolling from his mouth, and his nostrils smoking with the hot breaths that burst in streaming columns from them. Not until his swift career had brought him exactly in front of his position did the old man stir a muscle. But then, quick as the motion of the leaping game, his rifle jumped to his cheek, and even as the buck was at the central point of his leap, and suspended in the air, the piece cracked sharp and clear, and the deer, stricken to his death, fell with a crash to the ground. The quivering hounds rose to their feet, and bayed long and deep; Wild Bill swung his hat and yelled; and for a moment the woods rang with the wild cries of dogs and man.

"Lord-a-massy, Bill, what a mouth ye have when ye open it!" exclaimed the Trapper, as he leisurely poured the powder into the still smoking barrel. "Atween ye and the pups, it's enough to drive a man crazy. I should sartinly think ye had never seed a deer shot afore, by the way ye be actin'."

"I've seen a good many, as you know, John Norton; but I never saw one tumbled over by a single bullet when at the very top of his jump, as that one was. I surely thought you had waited too long, and I wouldn't have given a cent for your chances when you pulled. It was a wonderful shot, John Norton, and I would take just such another tramp as I have had, to see you do it again, old man."

"It wasn't bad," returned the Trapper; "no,

it sartinly wasn't bad, fur he was goin' as ef the Old Harry was arter him. I shouldn't wonder ef he had felt the tech of lead down there in the holler, and the smart of his hurt kept him flyin'. Let's go and look him over, and see ef we can't find the markin's of the bullit on him."

In a moment the two stood above the dead deer.

"It is as I thought," said the Trapper, as he pointed with his ramrod to a stain of blood on one of the hams of the buck. "The bullit drove through his thigh here, but it didn't tech the bone, and was a sheer waste of lead, fur it only sot him goin' like an arrer. Bill, I sartinly doubt," continued the old man, as he measured the noble animal with his eye, "I sartinly doubt ef I ever seed a bigger deer. There's seven prongs on his horns, and I'd bet a horn of powder agin a chargerful that he'd weigh three hundred pounds as he lies. Lord, what a Christmas gift he'll be fur the woman!

The skin will make a blanket fit fur a queen to sleep under, and the meat, jediciously cared for, will last her all winter. We must manage to git it to the edge of the clearin', anyhow, or the wolves might make free with our venison, Bill. Yer sled is a strong un, and it'll bear the loadin', ef ye go keerful."

The Trapper and his companion set themselves to their task with the energy of men accustomed to surmount every obstacle, and in a short half-hour the sled, with its double loading, stopped at the door of the lonely cabin.

"I don't understand this, Wild Bill," said the Trapper. "Here be a woman's tracks in the snow, and the door be left a leetle ajar, but there be no smoke in the chimney, and they sartinly ain't very noisy inside. I'll jest give a knock or two, and see ef they be stirrin';" and, suiting the action to the word, he knocked long and loud on the large door. But to his noisy summons there came no response, and without a moment of farther hesitation he shoved open the door, and entered.

"God of marcy! Wild Bill," exclaimed the Trapper, "look in here!"

A huge room dimly lighted, holes in the roof, here and there a heap of snow on the floor, an immense fireplace with no fire in it, and a group of scared, wild-looking children huddled together in the farther corner, like young and timid animals that had fled in affright from the nest where they had slept, at some fearful intrusion. That is what the Trapper saw.

"I" — Whatever Wild Bill was about to say, his astonishment, and we may add his pity, were too profound for him to complete his ejaculation.

"Don't ye be afeerd, leetle uns," said the Trapper, as he advanced into the centre of the room to more fully survey the wretched place. "This be Christmas morn, and me and Wild Bill and the pups have come over the mountain to wish ye all a merry Christmas. But where be yer mother?" queried the old man, as he looked kindly at the startled group.

"We don't know where she is," answered the older of the two girls; "we thought she was in bed with us, till you woke us. We don't know where she has gone."

"I have it, I have it, Wild Bill!" exclaimed the Trapper, whose eyes had been busy scanning the place while talking with the children. "The rifle be gone from the hangings, and the tracks in the snow be hern. Yis, yis, I see it all. She went out in hope of gittin' the leetle uns here somethin' to eat, and that was her rifle we heerd, and her bullet made that hole in the ham of the buck. What a disapp'intment to the poor creetur when she seed she hadn't hit him! Her heart eena'most broke, I dare say. But the Lord was in it — leastwise, he didn't go ag'in the proper shapin' of things arterwards. Come, Bill, let's stir round lively, and get the shanty in shape a leetle, and some vict'als on the table afore she comes. Yis, git out yer axe, and slash into that dead beech at the corner of the cabin, while I sorter clean up inside. A fire is the fust thing on sech a mornin' as this; so scurry round, Bill, and bring in the wood as ef ye was a good deal in 'arnest, and do ye cut to the measure of the fireplace, and don't waste yer time in shortenin' it, fur the longer the fireplace, the longer the wood; that is, ef ye want to make it a heater."

His companion obeyed with alacrity; and by the time the Trapper had cleaned out the snow, and swept down the soot from the sides of the fireplace, and put things partially to rights, Bill had stacked the dry logs into the huge opening, nearly to the upper jamb, and, with the help of some large sheets of birch-bark, kindled them to a flame. "Come here, leetle uns," said the Trapper, as he turned his good-natured face toward the children, — "come here, and put yer leetle feet on the h'arthstun, fur it's warmin', and I conceit yer toes be about freezin'."

It was not in the power of children to withstand the attraction of such an invitation, extended with such a hearty voice and such benevolence of feature. The children came promptly forward, and stood in a row on the great stone, and warmed their little shivering bodies by the abundant flames.

"Now, leetle folks," said the Trapper, "jest git yerselves well warmed, then git on what clothes ye've got, and we'll have some breakfast, — yis, we'll have breakfast ready by the time yer mother gits back, fur I know where she be gone, and she'll be hungry and cold when she gits in. I don't conceit that this little chap here can help much, but ye girls be big enough to help a good deal. So, when ye be warm, do ye put away the bed to the furderest corner, and shove out the table in front of the fire, and put on the dishes, sech as ye have, and be smart about it, too, fur yer mother will sartinly be comin' soon, and we must be ahead of her with the cookin'."

What a change the next half-hour made in the appearance of the cabin! The huge fire sent its heat to the farthest corner of the great room. The miserable bed had been removed out of sight, and the table, drawn up in front of the fire, was set with the needed dishes. On the hearthstone a large platter of venison steak, broiled by the Trapper's skill, simmered in the heat. A mighty pile of cakes, brown to a turn, flanked one side, while a stack of potatoes baked in the ashes supported the other. The teapot sent forth its refreshing odor through the room. The children, with their faces washed and hair partially, at least, combed, ran about with bare feet on the warm floor, comfortable and happy. To them it was as a beautiful dream. The breakfast was ready, and the visitors sat waiting for the coming of her to whose assistance the angel of Christmas Eve had sent them.

"Sh!" whispered the Trapper, whose quick

ear had caught the sound of a dragging step in the snow. "She's comin'!"

Too weary and faint, too sick at heart and exhausted in body to observe the unaccustomed signs of human presence around her dwelling, the poor woman dragged herself to the door, and opened it. The gun she still held in her hand fell rattling to the floor, and, with eyes wildly opened, she gazed bewildered at the spectacle. The blazing fire, the set table, the food on the hearthstone, the smiling children, the two men! She passed her hands across her eyes as one waking from sleep. Was she dreaming? Was this cabin the miserable hut she had left at daybreak? Was that the same fireplace in front of whose cold and cheerless recess she had crouched the night before? And were those two strangers there men, or were they angels? Was what she saw real, or was it only a fevered vision born of her weakness?

Her senses actually reeled to and fro, and she

trembled for a moment on the verge of unconsciousness. Indeed, the shock was so overwhelming that in another instant she would have swooned and fallen to the floor had not the growing faintness been checked by the sound of a human voice.

"A merry Christmas to ye, my good woman," said the Trapper. "A merry Christmas to ye and yourn!"

The woman started as the hearty tones fell on her ear, and, steadying herself by the door, she said, speaking as one partially dazed, —

"Are you John Norton the Trapper, or are you an ang —"

"Ye needn't sight agin," interrupted the old man. "Yis, I'm old John Norton himself, nothin' better and nothin' wuss; and the man in the chair here by my side is Wild Bill, and ye couldn't make an angel out of him, ef ye tried from now till next Christmas. Yis, my good woman, I'm John Norton, and this is Wild Bill, and we've come over the mountain to wish ye a merry Christmas, ye and yer leetle uns, and help ye keep the day; and, ye see, we've been stirrin' a leetle in yer absence, and breakfast be waitin'. Wild Bill and me will jest go out and cut a leetle more wood, while ye warm and wash yerself; and when ye be ready to eat, ye may call us, and we'll see which can git into the house fust."

So saying, the Trapper, followed by his companion, passed out of the door, while the poor woman, without a word, moved toward the fire, and, casting one look at her children, at the table, at the food on the hearthstone, dropped on her knees by a chair, and buried her face in her hands.

"I say," said Wild Bill to the Trapper, as he crept softly away from the door, to which he had returned to shut it more closely, "I say, John Norton, the woman is on her knees by a chair."

"Very likely, very likely," returned the old man reverently; and then he began to chop vigorously at a huge log, with his back toward his comrade.

Perhaps some of you who read this tale will come some time, when weary and heart-sick, to something drearier than an empty house, some bleak, cold day, some lonely morn, and with a starving heart and benumbed soul, — ay, and empty-handed, too, — enter in only to find it swept and garnished, and what you most needed and longed for waiting for you. Then will you, too, drop upon your knees, and cover your face with your hands, ashamed that you had murmured against the hardness of your lot, or forgotten the goodness of Him who suffered you to be tried only that you might more fully appreciate the triumph.

"My good woman," said the Trapper, when the breakfast was eaten, "we've come, as we said, to spend the day with you; and accordin' to custom — and a pleasant un it be fur sartin — we've brought ye some presents. A good many of them come from him who called on ye as he and me passed through the lake last fall. I dare say ye remember him, and he sartinly has remembered ye. Fur last evenin', when I was makin' up a leetle pack to bring ye myself, — fur I conceited I had better come over and spend the day with ye, — Wild Bill came to my door with a box on his sled that the boy had sent in from his home in the city; and in the box he had put a great many presents fur him and me; and in the lower half of the box he had put a good many presents fur ye and yer leetle uns, and we've brought them all over with us. Some of the things be fur eatin' and some of them be fur wearin'; and that there may be no misunderstandin', I would say that all the things that be in the pack-basket there, and all the things that be on the sled, too, belong to ye. And as I see the wood-pile isn't a very big un fur this time of the year, Bill and me be goin' out to settle our breakfast a leetle with the axes. And while we be gone, I conceit ye had better rummage the things over, and them that be good fur eatin' ye had better put in the cupboard, and them that be good fur wearin' ye had better put on yerself and yer leetle uns; and then we'll all be ready to make a fair start. Fur this be Christmas Day, and we be goin' to keep it as it orter be kept. Ef we've had sorrers, we'll forgit 'em; and we'll laugh, and eat, and be merry. Fur this be Christmas, my good woman! children, this be Christmas! Wild Bill, my boy, this be Christmas; and pups, this be Christmas! And we'll all laugh, and eat, and be merry."

The joyfulness of the old man was contagious. His happiness flowed over as waters flow over the rim of a fountain. Wild Bill laughed as he seized his axe, the woman rose from the table smiling, the girls giggled, the little boy stamped, and the hounds, catching the spirit of their merry master, swung their tails round, and bayed in canine gladness; and amid the joyful uproar the old Trapper spun himself out of the door, and chased Wild Bill through the snow like a boy.

The dinner was to be served at two o'clock; and what a dinner it was, and what preparations preceded! The snow had been shovelled from around the cabin, the holes in the roof roughly but effectually thatched. A good pile of wood was stacked in front of the doorway. The spring that bubbled from the bank had been cleared of ice, and a protection constructed over it. The huge buck had been dressed, and hung high above the reach of wolves. Cedar and balsam branches had been placed in the corners and along the sides of the room. Great sprays of the tasselled pine and the feathery tamarack were suspended from the ceiling. The table had been enlarged, and extra seats extemporized. The long-unused oven had been cleaned out, and under its vast dome the red flames flashed and rolled upward. What a change a few hours had brought to that lonely cabin and its wretched inmates! The woman, dressed in her new garments, her hair smoothly combed, her face lighted with smiles, looked positively comely. The girls, happy in their fine clothes and marvellous toys, danced round the room, wild with delight; while the little boy strutted about the floor in his new boots, proudly showing them to each person for the hundredth time.

The hostess's attention was equally divided between the temperature of the oven and the adornment of the table. A snow-white sheet, one of a dozen she had found in the box, was drafted peremptorily into service, and did duty as a tablecloth. Oh, the innocent and funny make-shifts of poverty, and the goodly distance it can make a little go! Perhaps some of us, as we stand in our rich dining-rooms, and gaze with pride at the silver, the gold, the cut-glass, and the transparent china, can recall a little kitchen in a homely house far away, where our good mothers once set their tables for their guests, and what a brave show the few extra dishes made when they brought them out on the rare festive days!

However it might strike you, fair reader, to the poor woman and her guests there was nothing incongruous in a sheet serving as a tablecloth. Was it not white and clean and properly shaped, and would it not have been a tablecloth if it hadn't been a sheet? How very nice and particular some people can be over the trifling matter of a name! And this sheet had no right to be a sheet; for any one with half an eye could see at a glance that it was predestined from the first to be a tablecloth, for it sat as smoothly on the wooden surface as pious looks on a deacon's face, while the easy and nonchalant way it draped itself at the corners was perfectly jaunty.

The edges of this square of white sheeting that had thus providentially found its true and predestined use were ornamented with the leaves of the wild myrtle, stitched on in the form of scallops. In the centre, with a brave show of artistic skill, were the words, "Merry Christmas," prettily worked with the small brown cones of the pines. This, the joint product of Wild Bill's industry and the woman's taste, commanded the enthusiastic admiration of all; and even the little boy, from the height of a chair into which he had climbed, was profoundly affected by the show it made.

The Trapper had charge of the meat department, and it is safe to say that no Delmonico could undertake to serve venison in greater variety than did he. To him it was a grand occasion, and — in a culinary sense — he rose grandly to meet it. What bosom is without its little vanities? and shall we laugh at the dear old man because he looked upon the opportunity before him with feeling other than pure benevolence, — even of complacency that what he was doing was being done as no one else could do it?

There was venison roasted, and venison broiled, and venison fried; there was hashed venison, and venison spitted; there was a side-dish of venison sausage, strong with the odor of sage, and slightly dashed with wild thyme; and a huge kettle of soup, on whose rich creamy surface pieces of bread and here and there a slice of potato floated.

"I tell ye, Bill," said the Trapper to his companion, as he stirred the soup with a long ladle, "this pot isn't actilly runnin' over with taters, but ye can see a bit occasionally ef ye look sharp and keep the ladle goin' round pretty lively. No, the taters ain't over-plenty," continued the old man, peering into the pot, and sinking his voice to a whisper, "but there wasn't but fifteen in the bag, and the woman took twelve of 'em fur her kittle, and ye can't make three taters look actilly crowded in two gallons of soup, can ye, Bill?" And the old man punched that personage in the ribs with the thumb of the hand that was free from service, while he kept the ladle going with the other.

"Lord!" exclaimed the Trapper, speaking to Bill, who, having taken a look into the old man's kettle, was digging his knuckles into his eyes to free them from the spray that was jetted into them from the fountains of mirth within that were now in full play, — "Lord! ef there isn't another piece of tater gone all to pieces! Bill, ef I make another circle with this ladle, there won't be a whole slice left, and ye'll swear there wasn't a tater in the soup." And the two men, with their faces within twenty inches, laughed and laughed like boys.

How sweet it is to think that when the Maker set up this strange instrument we call ourselves, and strung it for service, he selected of the heavy chords so few, and of the lighter ones so many! Some muffled ones there are; some slow and solemn sounds swell sadly forth at intervals, but blessed be God that we are so easily tickled, and the world is so funny that within it, even when exiled from home and friends, we find, as the days come and go, the causes and occasions of hilarity!

Wild Bill had been placed in charge of the liquids. What a satire there is in circumstances, and how those of to-day laugh at those of yesterday! Yes, Wild Bill had charge of the liquids, — no mean charge, when the occasion is considered. Nor was the position without its embarrassments, as few honorable positions are, for it brought him face to face with the problem of the day — dishes; for, between the two cooks of the occasion, every dish in the cabin had been brought into requisition, and poor Bill was left in the predicament of having to make tea and coffee with no pots to make them in.

But Bill was not lacking in wit, if he was in pots, and he solved the conundrum how to make tea without a teapot in a manner that extorted the woman's laughter, and commanded the old Trapper's admiration.

In ransacking the lofts above the apartment, he had lighted on several large, stone jugs, which, with the courage — shall we call it the audacity? — of genius, he had seized upon; and, having thoroughly rinsed them, and freed them from certain odors, — which we are free to say Bill was more or less familiar with, — he brought them forward as substitutes for kettle and pot. Indeed, they worked admirably, for in them the berry and the leaves might not only be properly steeped, but the flavor could be retained beyond what it might in many of our famous and high-sounding patented articles.

But Bill, while ingenious and courageous to the last degree, was lacking in education, especially in scientific directions. He had never been made acquainted with that great promoter of modern civilization — the expansive properties of steam. The corks he had whittled out for his bravely extemporized tea and coffee pots were of the closest fit; and, as they had been inserted with the energy of a man who, having conquered a serious difficulty, is determined to reap the full benefit of his triumph, there was at least no danger that the flavor of the concoctions would escape through any leakage at the muzzle. Having thus prepared them for steeping, he placed the jugs in his corner of the fireplace, and pushed them well up through the ashes to the live coals.

"Wild Bill," said the Trapper, who wished to give his companion the needed warning in as delicate and easy a manner as possible, "Wild Bill, ye have sartinly got the right idee techin' the makin' of tea and coffee, fur the yarb should be steeped, and the berry too, — leastwise, arter it's biled up once or twice, — and therefore it be only reasonable that the nozzles should be closed moderately tight; but a man wants considerable experience in the business, or he's likely to overdo it jest a leetle, and ef ye don't cut some slots in them wooden corks ye've driven into them nozzles, Bill, there'll be a good deal of tea and coffee floatin' round in your corner of the fireplace afore many minutes, and I conceit there'll be a man about your size lookin' for a couple of corks and pieces of jugs out there in the clearin', too."

"Do you think so?" answered Bill incredulously. "Don't you be scared, old man, but keep on stirring your soup and turning the meat, and I'll keep my eye on the bottles."

"That's right, Bill," returned the Trapper; "ye keep yer eye right on 'em, specially on that un that's furderest in toward the butt of the beech log there; fur ef there's any vartue in signs, that jug be gittin' oneasy. Yis," continued the old man, after a minute's pause, during which his eye hadn't left the jug, "yis, that jug will want more room afore many minutes, ef I'm any jedge, and I conceit I had better give it the biggest part of the fireplace;" and the Trapper hastily moved the soup and his half-dozen plates of cooked meats to the other end of the hearthstone, whither he retired himself, like one who, feeling that he is called upon to contend with unknown forces, wisely beats a retreat. He even put himself behind a stack of wood that lay piled up in his corner, like one who does not despise, in a sudden emergency, an artificial protection.

"Bill," called the Trapper, "edge round a leetle, — edge round, and git in closer to the jamb. It's sheer foolishness standin' where ye be, fur the water will be wallopin' in a minit, and ef the corks be swelled in the nozzle, there'll be an explosion. Git in toward the jamb, and watch the ambushment under kiver."

"Old man," answered Bill, as he turned his back carelessly toward the fireplace, "I've got the bearin's of this trail, and know what I'm about. The jugs are as strong as iron kittles, and I ain't afraid of their bust." —

Bill never finished the sentence, for the explosion predicted by the Trapper occurred. It was a tremendous one, and the huge fireplace was filled with flying brands, ashes, and clouds of steam. The Trapper ducked his head, the woman screamed, and the hounds rushed howling to the farthest end of the room; while Bill, with half a somersault, disappeared under the table.

"Hurrah!" shouted the Trapper, lifting his head from behind the wood, and critically surveying the scene. "Hurrah, Bill!" he shouted, as he swung the ladle over his head. "Come out from under the table, and man yer battery agin. Yer old mortars was loaded to the muzzle, and ef ye had depressed the pieces a leetle, ye'd 'a' blowed the cabin to splinters; as it was, the chimney got the biggest part of the chargin', and ye'll find yer rammers on the other side of the mountain."

It was, in truth, a scene of uproarious hilarity; for once the explosion was over, and the woman and children saw there was no danger, and apprehended the character of the performance, they joined unrestrainedly in the Trapper's laughter, in which they were assisted by Wild Bill, as if he were not the victim of his own over-confidence.

"I say, old Trapper," he called from under the table, "did both guns go off? I was gitting under cover when the battery opened, and didn't notice whether the firing was in sections or along the whole line. If there's a piece left, I think I will stay where I am; for I am in a good position to observe the range, and watch the effect of the shot. I say, hadn't you better get behind the wood-pile again?"

"No, no," interrupted the Trapper; "the whole battery went at the word, Bill, and there isn't a gun or a gun-carriage left in the casement. Ye've wasted a gill of the yarb, and a quarter of a pound of the berry; and ye must hurry up with another outfit of bottles, or we'll have nothin' but water to drink at the dinner."

The dinner! That great event of the day, the crown and diadem to its royalty, and which became it so well, was ready promptly to the hour. The table, enlarged as it was to nearly double its original dimensions, could scarcely accommodate the abundance of the feast. Ah, if some sweet power would only enlarge our hearts when, on festive days, we enlarge our tables, how many of the world's poor, that now go hungry while we feast, would then be fed!

At one end of the table sat the Trapper, Wild Bill at the other. The woman's chair was at the centre of one of the sides, so that she sat facing the fire, whose generous flames might well symbolize the abundance which amid cold and hunger had so suddenly come to her. On her right hand the two girls sat; on her left, the boy. A goodly table, a goodly fire, and a goodly company, — what more could the Angel of Christmas ask to see?

Thus were they seated, ready to begin the repast; but the plates remained untouched, and the happy noises which had to that moment filled the cabin ceased; for the Angel of Silence, with noiseless step, had suddenly entered the room. There's a silence of grief, there's a silence of hatred, there's a silence of dread; of these, men may speak, and these they can describe. But the silence of our happiness, who can describe that? When the heart is full, when the long longing is suddenly met, when love gives to love abundantly, when the soul lacketh nothing and is content, — then language is useless, and the Angel of Silence becomes our only adequate interpreter. A humble table, surely, and humble folk around it; but not in the houses of the rich or the palaces of kings does gratitude find her only home, but in more lowly abodes and with lowly folk — ay, and often at the scant table, too — she sitteth a perpetual guest. Was it memory? Did the Trapper at that brief moment visit his absent friend? Did Wild Bill recall his wayward past? Were the thoughts of the woman busy with sweet scenes of earlier days? And did memory, by thus reminding them of the absent and the past, of the sweet things that had been and were, stir within their hearts thoughts of Him from whom all gifts descend, and of His blessed Son, in whose honor the day was named?

O memory! thou tuneful bell that ringeth on forever, friend at our feasts, and friend, too, let us call thee, at our burial, what music can equal thine? For in thy mystic globe all tunes abide, — the birthday note for kings, the marriage peal, the funeral knell, the gleeful jingle of merry mirth, and those sweet chimes that float our thoughts, like fragrant ships upon a fragrant sea, toward heaven, — all are thine! Ring on, thou tuneful bell; ring on, while these glad ears may drink thy melody; and when thy chimes are heard by me no more, ring loud and clear above my grave that peal which echoes to the heavens, and tells the world of immortality, that they who come to mourn may check their tears, and say, " *Why do we weep? He liveth still!* "

"The Lord be praised fur his goodness!" said the Trapper, whose thoughts unconsciously broke into speech. "The Lord be praised fur his goodness, and make us grateful fur his past marcies, and the plenty that be here!" And looking down upon the viands spread before him, he added, "The Lord be good to the boy, and make him as happy in his city home as be they who be wearin' and eatin' his gifts in the woods!"

"Amen!" said the woman softly, and a grateful tear fell on her plate.

"A—hem!" said Wild Bill; and then looking down upon his warm suit, he lifted his voice, and bringing it out in a clear, strong tone, said, "*Amen! hit or miss!*"

At many a table that day more formal grace was said, by priest and layman alike, and at many a table, by lips of old and young, response was given to the benediction; but we doubt if over all the earth a more honest grace was said or assented to than the Lord heard from the cabin in the woods.

The feast and the merry-making now began. The old Trapper was in his best mood, and fairly bubbled over with humor. The wit of Wild Bill was naturally keen, and it flashed at its best as he ate. The children stuffed and laughed as only children on such an elastic occasion can. And as for the poor woman, it was impossible for her, in the midst of such a scene, to be otherwise than happy, and she joined modestly in the conversation, and laughed heartily at the witty sallies.

But why should we strive to put on paper the wise, the funny, and the pleasant things that were said, the exclamations, the laughter, the story, the joke, the verbal thrust and parry of such an occasion? These, springing from the centre of the circumstance, and flashed into being at the instant, cannot be preserved for after-rehearsal. Like the effervescence of champagne, they jet and are gone; their force passes away with the noise that accompanied its out-coming.

Is it not enough to record that the dinner

was a success, that the Trapper's meats were put upon the table in a manner worthy of his reputation, that the woman's efforts at pastry-making were generously applauded, and that Wild Bill's tea and coffee were pronounced by the hostess the best she had ever tasted? Perhaps no meal was ever more enjoyed, as certainly none was ever more heartily eaten.

The wonder and pride of the table was the pudding, — a creation of Indian-meal, flour, suet, and raisins, re-enforced and assisted by innumerable spicy elements supposed to be too mysterious to be grasped by the masculine mind. In the production of this wonderful centre-piece, — for it had been unanimously voted the place of honor, — the poor woman had summoned all the latent resources of her skill, and in reference to it her pride and fear contended, while the anxiety with which she rose to serve it was only too plainly depicted on her countenance. What if it should prove a failure? What if she had made a miscal-

culation as to the amount of suet required, — a point upon which she had been somewhat confused? What if the raisins were not sufficiently distributed? What if it wasn't done through, and should turn out pasty? Great heavens! The last thought was of so overwhelming a character that no feminine courage could encounter it. Who may describe the look with which she watched the Trapper as he tasted it, or the expression of relief which brightened her anxious face when he pronounced warmly in its favor?

"It's a wonderful bit of cookin'," he said, addressing himself to Wild Bill, "and I sartinly doubt ef there be anything in the settlements to-day that can equal it. There be jest enough of the suet, and there be a plum fur every mouthful; and it be solid enough to stay in the mouth ontil ye've had time to chew it, and git a taste of the corn, — and I wouldn't give a cent for a puddin' ef it gits away from yer teeth fast. Yis, it be a wonderful bit of cookin'," and, turning to the woman, he added, "ye may well be proud of it."

What higher praise could be bestowed? And as it was re-echoed by all present, and plate after plate was passed for a second filling, the dinner came to an end with the greatest good feeling and hilarity.

## IV.

"Now fur the sled!" exclaimed the Trapper, as he rose from the table. "It be a good many years since I've straddled one, but nothin' settles a dinner quicker, or suits the leetle folks better. I conceit the crust be thick enough to bear us up, and, ef it is, we can fetch a course from the upper edge of the clearin' fifty rods into the lake. Come, childun, git on yer mittens and yer tippets, and h'ist along to the big pine, and ye shall have some fun ye won't forgit ontil yer heads be whiter than mine."

It is needless to record that the children hailed with delight the proposition of the Trapper, or that they were at the appointed spot long before the speaker and his companion reached it with the sled.

"Wild Bill," said the Trapper, as they stood

on the crest of the slope down which they were to glide, " the crust be smooth as glass, and the hill be a steep un. I sartinly doubt ef mortal man ever rode faster than this sled'll be goin' by the time it gits to where the bank pitches into the lake; and ef ye should git a leetle careless in yer steerin', Bill, and hit a stump, I conceit that nothin' but the help of the Lord or the rottenness of the stump would save ye from etarnity."

Now, Wild Bill was blessed with a sanguine temperament. To him no obstacle seemed serious if bravely faced. Indeed, his natural confidence in himself bordered on recklessness, to which the drinking habits of his life had, perhaps, contributed.

When the Trapper had finished speaking, Bill ran his eye carelessly down the steep hillside, smooth and shiny as polished steel, and said, " Oh, this isn't anything extry for a hill. I've steered a good many steeper ones, and in nights when the moon was at the half, and the sled overloaded at that. It don't make any difference how fast you go," he added, "if you only keep in the path, and don't hit anything."

"That's it, that's it," replied the Trapper. "But the trouble here be to keep in the path, fur, in the fust place, there isn't any path, and the stumps be pretty thick, and I doubt ef ye can line a trail from here to the bank by the lake without one or more sudden twists in it, and a twist in the trail, goin' as fast as we'll be goin', has got to be taken jediciously, or somethin' will happen. I say, Bill, what p'int will ye steer fur?"

Wild Bill, thus addressed, proceeded to give his opinion touching the proper direction of the flight they were to make. Indeed, he had been closely examining the ground while the Trapper was speaking, and therefore gave his opinion promptly and with confidence.

"Ye have chosen the course with jedgment," said the old man approvingly, after he had studied the line his companion pointed out critically for a moment. "Yis, Bill, ye have a nateral eye for the business, and I sartinly have more confidence in ye than I had a minit ago, when ye was talkin' about a steeper hill than this; fur this hill drops mighty sudden in the pitches, and the crust be smooth as ice, and the sled'll go like a streak when it gits started. But the course ye've p'inted out be a good un, fur there be only one bad turn in it, and good steerin' orter put a sled round that. I say," continued the old man, turning toward his companion, and pointing out the crook in the course at the bottom of the second dip, "can ye swing around that big stump there without upsettin' when ye come to it?"

"Swing around? Of course I can," retorted Wild Bill positively. "There's plenty room to the left, and"—

"Ay, ay; there be plenty of room, as ye say, ef ye don't take too much of it," interrupted the Trapper. "But"—

"I tell you," broke in the other, "I'll turn

my back to no man in steering a sled; and I can put this sled, and you on it, around that stump a hundred times, and never lift a runner."

"Well, well," responded the Trapper, "have it your own way. I dare say ye be good at steerin', and I sartinly know I'm good at ridin'; and I can ride as fast as ye can steer, ef ye hit every stump in the clearin'. Now, childun," continued the old man, turning to the little group, "we be goin' to try the course; and ef the crust holds up, and Wild Bill keeps clear of the stumps, and nothin' onusual happens, ye shall have all the slidin' ye want afore ye go in. Come, Bill, git yer sled p'inted right, and I'll be gittin' on, and we'll see ef ye can steer an old man round a stump as handily as ye say ye can."

The directions of the Trapper were promptly obeyed, and in an instant the sled was in a right position, and the Trapper proceeded to seat himself with the carefulness of one who feels he is embarking on a somewhat uncertain venture, and has grave misgivings as to what will be the upshot of the undertaking. The sled was large and strongly built; and it added not a little to his comfort to feel that he could put entire confidence in the structure beneath them.

"The sled'll hold," he said to himself, "ef the loadin' goes to the jedgment."

The Trapper was no sooner seated than Wild Bill threw himself upon the sled, with one leg under him and the other stretched at full length behind. This was a method of steering that had come into vogue since the Trapper's boyhood, for in his day the steersman sat astride the sled, with his feet thrust forward, and steered by the pressure of either heel upon the snow.

"Hold on, Bill!" exclaimed the Trapper, whose eye this novel method of steering had not escaped. "Hold on, and hold up a minit. Heavens and 'arth! ye don't mean to steer this sled with one toe, do ye, and that, too, the length of a rifle-barrel astarn? Wheel round, and spread yer legs out as ye orter, and steer this sled in an honest fashion, or there'll be trouble aboard afore ye git to the bottom."

"Sit round!" retorted Bill. "How could I see to steer if I was sitting right back of you? For you're nigh a foot taller than I be, and your shoulders are as broad as the sled."

"Yer p'ints be well taken, fur sartin," replied the Trapper; "fur it be no more than reasonable that the man that steers should see where he be goin', and I am anxious as ye be that ye should. Yis, I sartinly want ye to see where ye be goin' on this trip, anyhow, fur the crew be a fresh un, and the channel be a leetle crooked. But be ye sartin, Bill, that ye can fetch round that stump there as it orter be did, with nothin' but yer toe out behind? It may be the best way, as ye say, but it don't look like honest steerin' to a man of my years."

"I have used both ways," answered Bill, "and I give you my word, old man, that this is the best one. You can git a big swing with your foot stretched out in this fashion, and the sled feels the least pressure of the toe. Yes, it's all right. John Norton, are you ready?"

"Yis, yis, as ready as I ever shall be," answered the Trapper, in a voice in which doubt and resignation were equally mingled. "It may be as ye say," he continued; "but the rudder be too fur behind to suit me, and ef anything happens on this cruise, jest remember, Wild Bill, that my jedgment"—

The sentence the Trapper was uttering was abruptly cut short at this point; for Bill had started the sled with a sudden push, and leaped to his seat behind the Trapper as it glided downward and away. In an instant the sled was under full headway, for the dip was a sharp one, and the crust smooth as ice. Scarce had it gone ten rods from the point where it started before it was in full flight, and was gliding downward with what would have been, to any but a man of the steadiest nerve, a frightful velocity. But the Trapper was of too cool and courageous temperament to be disturbed even by actual danger. Indeed, the swiftness of their downward career, as the sled with a buzz and a roar swept along over the resounding crust, stirred the old man's blood with a tingle of excitement; while the splendid manner with which Wild Bill was keeping it to the course settled upon filled him with admiration, and was fast making him a convert to the new method of steering.

Downward they flashed. The Trapper's cap had been blown from his head; and as the old man sat bolt-upright on his sled, his feet bravely planted on the round, his face flushed, and his white hair streaming, he looked the very picture of hearty enjoyment. Above his head the face of Wild Bill looked actually sharpened by the pressure of the air on either cheek as it clove through it; but his lips were bravely set, and his eyes were fastened without winking on the big stump ahead, toward which they were rushing.

It was at this point that Wild Bill vindicated his ability as a steersman, and at the same time barely escaped shipwreck. At the proper moment he swept his foot to the left, and the sled, in obedience to the pressure, swooped in that direction. But in his anxiety to give the stump a wide berth, Bill overdid the pressure that was needed a trifle; for in calculating the curve required he had failed to allow for the sidewise motion of the sled, and, instead of hitting one stump, it looked for an instant as if he would be precipitated among a dozen.

"Heave her starn up, Wild Bill! up with her starn, I say," yelled the Trapper, "or there won't be a stump left in the clearin'."

With a quickness and courage that would have done credit to any steersman, — for the speed at which they were going was terrific, — Bill swept his foot to the right, leaning his body well over at the same instant. The Trapper instinctively seconded his endeavors, and with hands that gripped either side of the sled he hung over that side which was upon the point of going into the air. For several rods the sled glided along on a single runner, and then, righting itself with a lurch, jumped the summit of the last dip, and raced away, like a swallow in full flight, toward the lake.

Now, at the edge of the clearing that bounded the shore was a bank of considerable size. Shrubs and stunted bushes fringed the crest of it. These had been buried beneath the snow, and the crust had formed smoothly over them; and as it was upheld by no stronger support than such as the hidden shrubbery furnished, it was incapable of sustaining any considerable pressure.

Certainly no sled was ever moving faster than was Wild Bill's, when it came to this point; and certainly no sled ever stopped quicker, for the treacherous crust dropped suddenly under it, and the sled was left with nothing but the hind part of one of the runners sticking up in sight. But though the sled was suddenly checked in its career, the Trapper and Wild Bill continued their flight. The former slid from the sled without meeting any obstruction, and with the same velocity with which he had been moving. Indeed, so little was his position changed, that one almost might fancy that no accident had happened, and that the old man was gliding forward to the end of the course with an adequate structure under him. But with the latter it was far different; for, as the sled stopped, he was projected sharply upward into the air, and, after turning several somersaults, he actually landed in front of the Trapper, and glided along on the slippery surface ahead of him. And so the two men shot onward, one after the other, while the children cackled from the hill-top, and the woman swung her bonnet over her head, and laughed from her position in the doorway.

"Bill," called the Trapper, when by dint of

much effort they had managed to check their motion somewhat, "Bill, ef the cruise be about over, I conceit we'd better anchor hereabouts. But I shipped fur the voyage, and ye be capt'in, and as ye've finally got the right way to steer, I feel pretty safe techin' the futur."

It was not until they had come to a full stop, and looked around them, that they realized the distance they had come; for they had in truth slid nearly across the bay.

"I've boated a good many times on these waters, and under sarcumstances that called fur 'arnest motion, but I sartinly never went across this bay as fast as I've did it to-day. How do ye feel, Bill, how do ye feel?"

"A good deal shaken up," was the answer, "a good deal shaken up."

"I conceit as much," answered the Trapper, "I conceit as much, fur ye left the sled with mighty leetle deliberation; and when I saw yer legs comin' through the air, I sartinly doubted ef the ice would hold ye. But ye steered with jedgment; yis, ye steered with jedgment, Bill; and I'd said it ef we'd gone to the bottom."

The sun was already set when they returned to the cabin; for, selecting a safer course, they had given the children an hour's happy sliding. The woman had prepared some fresh tea and a lunch, which they ate with lessened appetites, but with humor that never flagged. When it was ended, the old Trapper rose to depart, and with a dignity and tenderness peculiarly his own, thus spoke:—

"My good woman," he said, "the moon will soon be up, and the time has come fur me to be goin'. I've had a happy day with ye and the leetle uns; and the trail over the mountain will seem shorter, as the pups and me go home, thinkin' on't. Wild Bill will stay a few days, and put things a leetle more to rights, and git up a wood-pile that will keep ye from choppin' fur a good while. It's his own thought, and ye can thank him accordin'ly." Then, having kissed each of the children, and spoken a few words to Wild Bill, he took the woman's hand, and said, —

"The sorrers of life be many, but the Lord never forgits. I've lived ontil my head be whitenin', and I've noted that though he moves slowly, he fetches most things round about the time we need 'em; and the things that be late in comin', I conceit we shall git somewhere furder on. Ye didn't kill the big buck this mornin', but the meat ye needed hangs at yer door, nevertheless." And, shaking the woman heartily by the hand, he whistled to the hounds, and passed out of the door. The inmates of the cabin stood and watched him, until, having climbed the slope of the clearing, he disappeared in the shadows of the forest; and then they closed the door. But more than once Wild Bill noted that as the woman stood wiping her dishes, she wiped her eyes as well; and more than once he heard her say softly to herself. "God bless the dear old man!"

Ay, ay, poor woman, we join thee in thy prayer. God bless the dear old man! and not only him, but all who do the deeds he did. God bless them one and all!

Over the crusted snow the Trapper held his course, until he came, with a happy heart, to his cabin. Soon a fire was burning on his own hearthstone, and the hounds were in their accustomed place. He drew the table in front, where the fire's fine light fell on his work, and, taking some green vines and branches from the basket, began to twine a wreath. One he twined, and then he began another; and often, as he twined the fadeless branches in, he paused, and long and lovingly looked at the two pictures hanging on the wall; and when the wreaths were twined, he hung them on the frames, and, standing in front of the dumb reminders of his absent ones, he said, "*I miss them so!*"

Ah! friend, dear friend, when life's glad day with you and me is passed, when the sweet

Christmas chimes are rung for other ears than ours, when other hands set the green branches up, and other feet glide down the polished floor, may there be those still left behind to twine us wreaths, and say, " *We miss them so!* "

And this is the way John Norton the Trapper kept his Christmas.

www.ingramcontent.com/pod-product-compliance
Lightning Source LLC
Chambersburg PA
CBHW031343160426
43196CB00007B/724